THE URBANA FREE LIBRARY

3 1230 00964 2287

DISCARDED BY THE
URBANA FREE LIBRARY

D1212905

The Urbana Free Library

To renew: call **217-367-4057**
or go to **urbanafreelibrary.org**
and select **My Account**

The **Sophia Day**® Creative Team-
Megan Johnson, Stephanie Strouse,
Kayla Pearson, Timothy Zowada, Mel Sauder

A SPECIAL THANK YOU to our team of reviewers who graciously give us
feedback, edits and help our products remain genuinely diverse.

© 2019 MVP Kids Media, LLC, all rights reserved

No part of this publication may be reproduced in whole or in part by
any mechanical, photographic or electronic process, or in the form of
any audio or video recording nor may it be stored in a retrieval system
or transmitted in any form or by any means now known or hereafter
invented or otherwise copied for public or private use without the written
permission of MVP Kids Media, LLC.
For more information regarding permission, visit our website at
www.MVPKids.com.

Published and Distributed by MVP Kids Media, LLC
Mesa, Arizona, USA
Printed by RR Donnelley Asia Printing Solutions, Ltd
Dongguan City, Guangdong Province, China
DOM Jan 2019, Job # 02-005-01

Look for 'Playful Curiosity'
(Yong's imaginary monkey sidekick)
He'll help you break out of the
boredom box, too. You never
know where he might show up!

help **me** UNDERSTAND™

Feeling **Bored** &
Learning **Curiosity**™

REAL

mvpkids®

Yong Breaks Out
of the
Boredom Box

SOPHIA DAY®

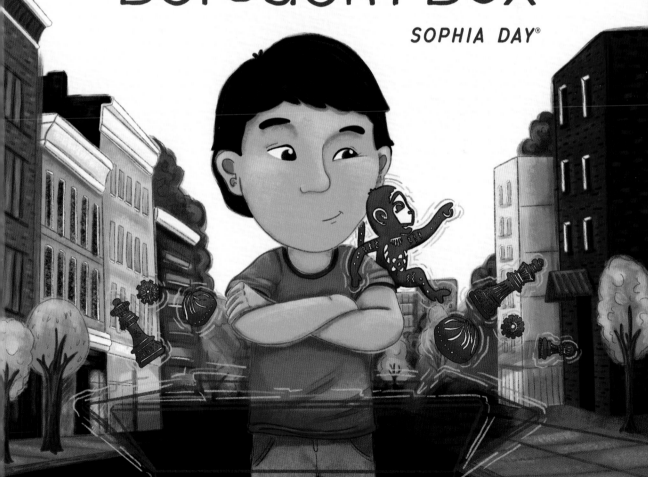

Written by Megan Johnson *Illustrated by* Stephanie Strouse

Yong closed his book. He stared out the window and sighed. Today was just the same as every other.

He was sitting in
the family restaurant
finishing homework
with his sister... again.
He felt like he lived his whole life
in a **tiny little box.**

Lily completed her worksheet and packed her school books away.

She tied her apron around her waist.

Unlike Yong, Lilly enjoyed helping out after school.

"At least she likes her chores," he thought. Lilly loved to check on the customers and refill their drinks.

Jun and Li's Chinatown

Yong stood up to start his chores. He dragged his feet to get the menus.

As he wiped them off he wondered, "Why do I have to do all the *boring* jobs?"

Next, he fed the fish.

"I do the same things every day. I wish I could do something fun," he complained to the goldfish. "But I guess you're just stuck in a box, too."

After his chores were done, Yong began to fidget. He wiped some dust off the bamboo plant.

He looked out the window at the Kung Fu studio across the street. He wished it were his day for lessons.

Yong had a hard time entertaining himself. He didn't mean to, but sometimes he got into trouble when he didn't have something to do.

Gong-Gong called from the kitchen, "Are you finished, Yong? I can find more work for you to do around here."

"No thanks," Yong answered. "I'm going to play upstairs. I don't know how you can work so hard all day. Isn't it boring?"

"I'm happy to cook all day. If it were boring, I would do it because I must work to make a living. But when you enjoy what you're doing, it doesn't feel like work at all."

"Boredom isn't about what is going on around you. It's an attitude within you. You must learn to entertain yourself rather than always being entertained.

With **curiosity** and a bit of creativity, anything can become play."

"Thanks Gong-Gong," Yong smiled.

"Mom, may I go upstairs?" Yong asked.

"Yes, but clean your room before dinner," his mom agreed.

Yong sighed. "Okay." He was glad to go upstairs, but cleaning his room was just one more boring thing to do.

It was convenient that they lived in an apartment above the restaurant, but it made Yong's world feel even smaller.

Yong tossed his bag into his room and fell onto the couch.

He turned on his favorite show.
He had already seen every episode.
"There's *nothing* to do. This is *boring*,"
he thought. Yong picked up his tablet and
scrolled through his games.
"I'm tired of these."

Yong peeked into his bedroom and sighed. "Cleaning is boring, too, but it has to be done," he told himself.

He stepped on something as he entered his messy room. "On no!" he cried. "My bank!"

It had been a gift from his aunt in China. Yong liked how a little monkey peeked out of the box and grabbed coins.

"I'll ask her to bring me another one next time she comes," he thought.

As he went to set it on the dresser, he stubbed his toe on his tool set.

"Ouch!" he exclaimed.

Suddenly, he had an idea!

His dad was great at fixing things; maybe the bank wasn't forever broken. He finished picking up the bank and set it aside for later.

Yong straightened his sheets, then he put all of the toys onto his bed and began sorting them.

He almost forgot to feel bored as he paid attention to the things he was organizing.

"I've been missing this book!" he exclaimed. "Now all my action figures are together again!"

"There's the missing piece of my chess set!"

He felt like he was on a treasure hunt!

Now he needed to take care of the clothes
on his floor. Yong never liked doing laundry.
He remembered Gong-Gong's words,
"When you enjoy what you're doing
it doesn't feel like work."

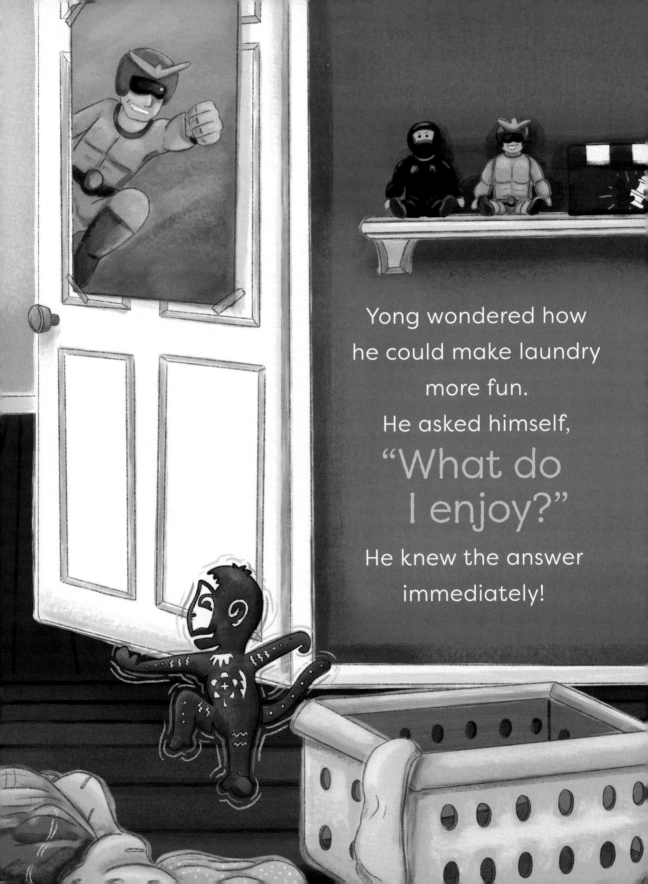

Yong wondered how
he could make laundry
more fun.
He asked himself,
"What do
I enjoy?"
He knew the answer
immediately!

He picked up a shirt and launched it forward with a **straight punch.**

He scooped a pair of pants onto his foot and shouted, **"back kick!"**

Yong carried his full basket downstairs to the laundry room in his building. He closed the machine with another palm strike!

Yong imagined how other kids might pick up their clothes.

Some could do a ballerina plié to drop their shirt in a basket.

Others might race a sibling to see who could fill their hamper first.

There are lots of ways to make simple tasks more fun! Yong had a new feeling. Instead of being bored and angry about his chores, he felt **creative and satisfied.**

That night at dinner Yong explained everything he had done. He told his mom how he paid attention to his things as he put them away.

"We can play chess again, and I even have a project for dad to help me with when he gets home," he said, thinking of his broken bank box.

"Well done," Gong-Gong said. "You did a good job with the things you were told to do. Now, you need to learn to **take initiative.** That means you try to do something you haven't been asked to do. There's always something to do if you look around."

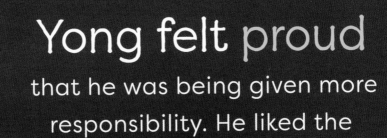

Yong felt proud

that he was being given more responsibility. He liked the challenge of finding things to do without being told.

The next day after school, Yong finished his homework in the restaurant as usual. He wiped the menus. He fed the fish.

He was right back in his usual boredom box.

He wished he was doing something fun.

Then he remembered that boredom is not about what goes on around him, but what goes on in his mind.

So Yong found something
interesting to think about
while he did his daily chores.

He thought about his broken bank.
He hoped he and Dad could fix it this weekend.
He remembered the treasures he found while
cleaning his room.

Something caught his eye and he remembered what Gong-Gong said about finding something to do.

He got an idea

and quickly ran upstairs to grab something.

"You're being very mysterious," Gong-Gong said as Yong rushed back in holding his supplies.

"I have an idea," Yong replied. "You'll see."

Yong stayed in the back room
all afternoon instead of going
upstairs to play.

When they sat down
for their dinner,
Mom was surprised.

"Wow!
What's the occasion,
Lily?" she asked.

"It wasn't me,"
Lily replied.

"It was me!"
Yong smiled proudly.
"I saw that the napkins
needed to be folded
and decided to try
something new."

Gong-Gong smiled,
proud that Yong had
taken initiative.

Gong-Gong was right - he could turn any work into play by combining it with something he enjoyed!

Yong no longer felt like he lived in a box. His **curiosity** opened up the whole world, and he could imagine fun into anything!

Every day feels just the same-
all your life contained
inside a tiny little box,
waiting to be entertained.

"I'm bored," you sigh and daydream.
"What can I do?" you ask.
But all the good suggestions
seem another boring task.

Each feeling has a purpose
and boredom has one, too-
to help you spend your time
on what is meaningful to you!

Some things must be done
but you can find a better way.
A little creativity
turns any chore into play!

Take up the responsibility;
find something helpful to do.
Challenge yourself to something big.
Learn to do something new!

Boredom isn't what's around you;
it's all inside your thoughts.
Curiosity and initiative
break you out of the boredom box!

LEARN & DISCUSS

Yong wants to talk about what he learned to break out of his boredom box. He started to understand how to handle his feelings of boredom, and he wants you to learn too!

"Like all feelings, boredom has a purpose. One purpose of boredom is to help you become curious. When you become curious you start to notice things you don't notice when you are entertained. If you are used to spending a lot of time being entertained by electronics, it might take some time for you to retrain your brain to think creatively."

How much free time do you have each day that is not spent on electronics?

Does this give you enough time to think creatively?

When can you set aside time to develop creativity?

"Like Gong-Gong said, 'With curiosity and a bit of creativity, anything can become play.' I practiced Kung Fu while picking up my laundry and had a lot of fun!"

You can find a way to enjoy just about anything that must be done:

- Think of three things you do not like to do.

- Now think of three things you DO like to do.

Can you find a way to combine something you do like with something you don't?

> "Sometimes boredom signals us to find something more meaningful to do with our time. I was bored watching the same TV show and playing the same games, so I cleaned my room instead. I didn't love cleaning, but it was satisfying to find toys that had been lost or forgotten."

When do you most often get bored?

How can you find meaning in tasks that seem boring?

Finish what is necessary, then take the initiative to do something that you find meaningful. What is meaningful to you?

> "A hobby that creates something, such as making crafts or contributes to daily life, such as setting a table nicely, is called a productive pastime. It is a way of entertaining yourself while also helping yourself or others with something meaningful. Gong-Gong enjoys cooking and uses that hobby to make a living. Some can find ways to turn a productive pastime into our life's work! I used origami to fold napkins, doing something I loved while also being helpful!"

How much of your free time is spent on productive pastimes?

What kinds of helpful hobbies might you enjoy?

What do you want to do when you grow up? How can you spend your free time preparing for a job you might want some day?

If you could design your dream job, what would it be?

> "Once you have thought about a meaningful purpose, you need to take initiative and do the first thing that works toward a new goal. To take initiative means to do something on your own without being told."

Here are some examples of ways you can take initiative:

- Look around your home for something that needs to be done and do it without being told.

- Find a book at the library or take a class about a topic that interests you.

- Ask a friend or trusted adult to teach you about their work or hobbies.

How can you help your child break out of the boredom box?

Kids are usually good at coming up with something to do, but they need unstructured time to practice this skill. Try to give children free time each day and resist the urge to tell them what to do during this time. If necessary, help your child come up with a list of activities they can choose during this time.

If your child can read, they have access to entertainment through books. Engage your child in a new book by reading the beginning of the book aloud. Once they've become intrested in the story line, get back to your own work or free time and encourage your child to finish the book on their own.

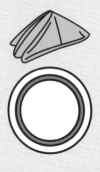

Your child might become easily bored when they are ready for a greater challenge or responsibility. True satisfaction comes from being helpful and productive, so give your child opportunities to complete daily chores. Don't assume that your child will not enjoy the activity. Some kids get great satisfaction out of setting a table or cleaning a bathroom. As your child gets older, help them find pastimes that prepare them for a career they might enjoy some day.

If your child has difficulty finding ways to safely entertain himself, consider these factors:

• Often when a child is whiny, they are signaling a need for connection. Give your child five minutes of focused interaction. Play a game together, push her on a swing or take a walk. After their needs for connection have been met they're more likely to be able to find their own entertainment for a while.

• Children need to be physically active to be able to concentrate. Make sure your child has had active play time, preferably outside, before expecting sustained focus on a sedentary activity.

• Television and other electronics have an addictive effect. It is harder for children to entertain themselves when they are accustomed to the entertainment of a screen. Cut back electronics to give your child's brain a chance to retrain its creativity.

• Consider the attitude with which you approach your daily tasks. Model making chores enjoyable by setting them to music, offering a reward afterward or completing a task in a playful way.

Research shows these amazing benefits of boredom and free play:

• Boredom can help children tune in to their inner thoughts and feelings as well as the world around them.

• Unstructured play time helps a person discover their true interests.

• Unstructured play gives children an opportunity to develop their decision-making and problem-solving skills.

• Boredom can force children to take initiative to do things on their own and become more assertive.

Meet the

mvpkids®

featured in

Yong Breaks Out of the Boredom Box™

YONG CHEN

Can you also find these MVP Kids®?

FAITH JORDAN

LEO RUSSO

FRANKIE RUSSO

Also featuring...

MR. HUANG CHEN
"Dad"

MRS. LI CHEN
"Mom"

LILLY CHEN
Sister

MR. JUN WANG
"Gong-Gong"
Grandfather

'PLAYFUL CURIOSITY'
Can you find Yong's imaginary
monkey sidekick throughout
the book?

Grow up with our **mvp**kids®

CELEBRATE!™
A **Preschool** Series
Ages 0-6

Our **CELEBRATE™** board books for toddlers and preschoolers focus on social, emotional, educational and physical needs. Helpful Teaching Tips are included in each book to equip parents to guide their children deeper into the subject of the book.

help me™ BECOME
Early Elementary
Ages 4-10

Our **Help Me Become™** series for early elementary readers tells three short stories of our MVP Kids® inspiring character growth. The stories each conclude with a discussion guide to help the child process the story and apply the concepts.

Don't miss out on our 3-part STAND anti-bullying series!

help me UNDERSTAND™
Elementary
Ages 6-12

Help your children grow in understanding all kinds of emotions by collecting the entire **Help Me Understand™** series!

Lucas Tames the Anger Dragon
SOPHIA DAY

Our **Help Me Understand™** series for elementary readers shares the stories of our MVP Kids® learning to understand and manage a specific emotion. Readers will gain tools to take responsibility for their own emotions and develop healthy relationships.

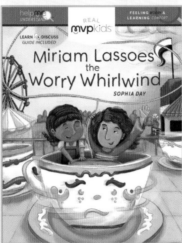

Miriam Lassoes the Worry Whirlwind
SOPHIA DAY

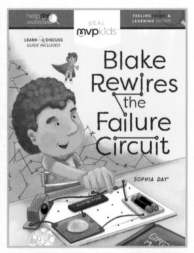

Blake Rewires the Failure Circuit
SOPHIA DAY™

Sarah Sizes Up the Insecure Ant
SOPHIA DAY™

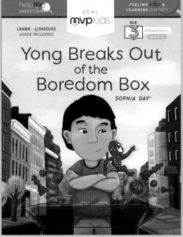

Yong Breaks Out of the Boredom Box
SOPHIA DAY™

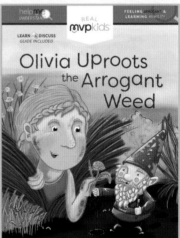

Olivia Uproots the Arrogant Weed

www.mvpkids.com

YONG CHEN

LEO RUSSO

FRANKIE RUSSO

JULIA ROJAS

AANYA PATEL

GABBY GONZALEZ

ANNIE JAMES

BLAKE JAMES

SARAH COHEN-GOLDSTEIN